Dealing
with Difficult
People

"Just as some people bring out your best, and other people bring out your worst, you can bring out the best in other people at their worst. It's a matter of understanding where they are coming from and what is likely to work with them."

"Communication is like a phone number. If you leave one number out, (only ten percent of the number), the call will not go through. If you dial the area code at the end as an after-thought, the call does not get through. You need all the digits to get through, and you need them in the right order."

"Just as surely as some people bring out your best and others bring out your worst, you can be one of the few who brings out the best in others at their worst. It's a matter of stabilizing yourself when dealing with them, understanding the positive intent behind their bad behavior, identifying a direction and organizing your own behavior around that direction."

Dealing with Difficult People

✔ **24 Lessons for Bringing Out the Best in Everyone**

RICK BRINKMAN
RICK KIRSCHNER

McGraw-Hill

New York Chicago San Francisco Lisbon
London Madrid Mexico City Milan New Delhi
San Juan Seoul Singapore Sydney Toronto

Contents

Dealing with Difficult People

☑ Dealing with difficult people

Difficult people: they're those people you can't stand and who don't do what you want them to do or do what you don't want them to do—and you don't know what to do about them!

Good news: you don't have to be their victim anymore. And while you can't change difficult people, you can communicate with them in such a way that they change themselves.

In this book, we define the four key areas you'll have to focus on to solve your people problems.

First, we'll describe the "10 most unwanted" types of behavior and examine the forces that compel people to be difficult in such a variety of ways. Then we'll help you build a "lens" for understanding why people act the way they do. Your ability to recognize the four key behavioral intentions is the first step toward success in influencing people to change their behavior toward the positive.

Then, we'll focus on surviving through skillful communication. This involves, among other things, learning the critical skills of *blending* and *redirecting*. We'll show you techniques that will help you listen to understand—and thereby to reach a deeper understanding. We'll suggest ways that you can speak to be understood. With effective listening skills and speaking skills in your repertoire, you'll have the building blocks for specific strategies for the toughest behaviors. And as you make these positive communication skills a habit, you will be able to prevent many of the difficult behaviors from ever occurring.

After that, we discuss each of the 10 most unwanted behaviors and tell you how to get the best result with each of them. We close by simply encouraging you to get started and suggesting some concrete action steps that you can take, *immediately*, to start dealing better with the people you can't stand.

So who are "we"? We are best friends, business partners, and physicians. We have spent many years studying health from an attitudinal and behavioral point of view. Long ago we became convinced that when people clarify their values, update their concepts, learn effective communication and relaxation skills, and define and work to meet their goals, they *feel* better. And as their mental and emotional health improves, many of their physical symptoms disappear.

In 1982, a mental health organization asked us to create a program on how to deal with difficult people. That marked the beginning of the process that resulted in this book—and also changed the way we define what we do. We now view all our work as public practice, supporting the health and well-being of people by educating them in some essential life skills, while getting a kind of continuing education in people for ourselves. For almost two decades, we've been learning about people's hopes and fears, how people build their lives or destroy them, how people communicate, what makes people difficult, and how best to deal with people at their worst.

We've written this book to pass that information along to you. We've presented these ideas to hundreds of thousands of people, through books, tapes, and seminars. We hope and believe that the ideas in this book will make a meaningful and lasting difference in the quality of your life.

There are difficult people and everyone has to deal with them: We identify 10 general types of troublesome behavior. You may have your own "least favorites."

There are effective ways to deal with these people: That's what this book is all about.

"This book will help you to identify and assemble elements of effective communication. You can get through and be one of the few who brings out the best in most people at their worst."

☐ Avoid or ignore difficult people

☑ Recognize the 10 most unwanted behaviors

What are the 10 most unwanted behaviors? We all answer this question slightly differently, depending on our own interpersonal strengths and weaknesses. But we would generally agree about which people are difficult and what they do that makes them difficult. We've identified 10 specific behavior patterns that sane people resort to when they feel threatened or thwarted, that represent their struggle with (or withdrawal from) undesired circumstances.

The Tank: Pushy and ruthless, loud and forceful, or with the quiet intensity and surgical precision of a laser, the Tank assumes that the end justifies the means. If you are in the way, you will be eliminated.

The Sniper: This covert operator resents you for some reason. Instead of getting mad, he or she gets even by identifying your weaknesses and using them against you, through sabotage, gossip and putdowns.

The Grenade: This person explodes in tantrums that seem disproportionate to the present circumstances, sending others ducking for cover and wondering what it's all about.

The Know-It-All: This person knows 98% of everything. (Just ask!) Know-It-Alls will tell you what they know—for hours at a time!—but won't take a moment to listen to your "clearly inferior ideas."

The Think-They-Know-It-All: Although these people don't know that much, they don't let that get in the way. If you don't know much about what they're talking about, they may mislead you into trouble or throw a project off track.

The Yes Person: Quick to agree, slow to deliver, the Yes Person leaves a trail of unfulfilled commitments and broken promises. Although they please no one, Yes People over-commit to please.

The Maybe Person: When faced with a crucial decision, the Maybe Person keeps putting it off until it's too late. Finally, there comes a point when the decision makes itself. Then it's nobody's default but his or her own.

The Nothing Person: You can't know what's going on because the Nothing Person tells you nothing—no feedback, verbal or nonverbal.

The No Person: This person says, "Every silver cloud has a dark lining" and "I'm not being negative, I'm being realistic." Doleful and discouraging, the No Person drives others to despair.

The Whiner: These people wallow in their woe, whine incessantly, and drag others down with the weight of their generalizations that nothing is right, everything is wrong, and it's always going to be that way unless you do something.

Some initial ideas for dealing with the 10 most unwanted types:

Understand that everybody reacts differently to these types of behavior: The person who's most irritating to you may be perfectly acceptable to someone else.

Get to know these types: Each warrants a different response. Think about the people around you. Does anybody at work or at home fit one of these descriptions?

Recognize the part you play: We can all be difficult at times. Understanding these behaviors in yourself will help you in your success with others.

"There is a certain consensus in polite society about who difficult people are and what it is they do that others find difficult."

☐ ~~React instinctively~~

☑ Choose your approach

Before we go any further, we need to stress the fact that there are at least four choices when dealing with people you can't stand. There's no magic formula; you are the best judge of which choice is right in any particular situation—although, as you'll see, we believe the first of these four choices is in fact a non-choice.

The four choices are:

Stay and do nothing. Doing nothing is not necessarily complete passivity; it may include both suffering and complaining to other people who can do nothing. Doing nothing is dangerous, because frustration with difficult people tends to build up and get worse over time. And complaining to people who can do nothing tends to lower morale and productivity, while postponing effective action.

Vote with your feet. Sometimes, your best option is to walk away. Not all situations are resolvable, and some are just not worth resolving. Voting with your feet makes sense when it no longer makes any sense to continue to deal with the person. If the situation is deteriorating, if everything you say or do makes matters worse, and if you find yourself losing control, remember that discretion is the better part of valor. Then walk away. Like Eleanor Roosevelt said, "No one can make you feel inferior without your permission." Before you decide to walk, however, you may want to consider your two other choices.

Change your attitude. Even if the difficult person continues to engage in the difficult behavior, you can learn to see the person differently, listen to the person differently, and feel differently about the person. There are attitudinal changes that you can make in yourself that will set you free from your reactions to problem people.

Change your behavior. When you change the way you deal with difficult people, they have to learn new ways to deal with you. There are effective, learnable strategies for dealing with most problem behaviors. That's what this book is about.

To summarize:

Realize that difficult behaviors fit into types, but each situation is different: You need to decide what kind of response is called for in each situation.

Avoid trying to do nothing: That strategy is probably not sustainable. If the situation is bad enough, you'll probably have to act.

Change your attitude first, then your behavior: Sometimes an attitude change alone is enough. But it's *always* a prerequisite for the harder task of changing your behavior.

"Don't despair. Remember that when dealing with difficult people, you always have a choice. In fact, you have four choices."

☐ Don't worry about motives

☑ Understand the four intents

The first step in changing your attitude toward the 10 most unwanted behaviors is to understand them. The key is the four intentions with which people respond to situations and in two variables: *assertiveness level* and *focus of attention*.

People range from passive (less assertive) to aggressive (more assertive). The assertiveness level is often influenced by the situation: during times of challenge, difficulty, or stress, people tend to move out of their normal "comfort zone" and become either more passive or more aggressive.

The focus of attention in a situation can be primarily on the task at hand—a *task* focus—or primarily on relationships—a *people* focus. In times of difficulty or stress, most people focus more on either the "what" (task) or the "who" (people) of the situation.

Now put the two variables together. A person can focus on *people* aggressively (e.g., belligerence), assertively (e.g., involvement), or passively (e.g., submission) or on a *task* aggressively (e.g., bold determination), assertively (e.g., involvement), or passively (e.g., withdrawal).

We each have a comfort zone of normal—more or less acceptable—behavior that challenges, difficulty, or stress can cause us to leave for a zone of exaggerated—or problem—behavior.

Every behavior (whether acceptable or problem) has a primary intent or purpose that it's trying to accomplish. We've identified four general intents that determine how people will react in any situation:

■ Get the task done.
■ Get the task right.
■ Get along with people.
■ Get appreciation from people.

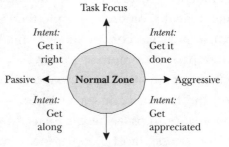

(These aren't the only intentions that motivate people, but they serve as a useful framework for understanding and dealing with difficult behaviors.)

When these intents become thwarted or frustrated, trouble arises. Behaviors can be pushed to the extreme—which may lead to the difficult behaviors outlined earlier.

The following diagram shows how the four intents relate to the four behaviors.

Intents are constantly shifting, depending on the person and situation, which brings changes in behavior. So you should:

Understand the four intents: They all have their time and place in our lives. When we keep them in balance, the result is often more success and less stress.

Be attentive to communication patterns (words, tone, and body language): They reveal the primary intent of difficult people and indicate how to deal with them.

Don't be difficult: When your intents are thwarted, you may become a difficult person. The more you know about why people behave as they do, the more you can change yourself.

"Have you ever been astonished at how quickly a person's behavior can change from one moment to the next?"

☑ Understand the first intent: get it done

Have you ever needed to get something done, finished, and behind you? When you need to *get it done*, you focus on the task at hand. And when you *really* need to get it done, you speed things up, focus on action, and assert yourself. You may even become careless and aggressive, leaping before you look or speaking without thinking. The people around you become peripheral.

When this attempt to get things done is frustrated, it can distort people's perceptions of a given situation. Suddenly, others appear to be wasting time, going off on tangents, or just plain taking too long. *The intent increases in intensity and the subsequent behavior becomes more controlling*.

The three most difficult controlling behaviors are found in the Tank, the Sniper, and the Know-It-All.

The Tank. On a mission to get things done, the Tank is unable to slow down and may push you around or run right over you in the process. The Tank has no inhibitions about ripping you apart personally, yet it's nothing personal: you just happened to get in the way. In an effort to control the process and accomplish the mission, Tank behavior ranges from mild pushiness to outright aggression.

The Sniper. When things aren't getting done to his or her satisfaction, the Sniper attempts to control you through embarrassment and humiliation. Most people live in fear of public embarrassment—a fact that Snipers use to their advantage, by making loaded statements and sarcastic comments at times when you are most vulnerable.

The Know-It-All. The Know-It-All controls people and events by dominating the conversation with lengthy, imperious arguments and eliminates opposition by finding flaws and weaknesses to discredit other points of view. Because Know-It-Alls are actually knowledgeable and competent, most people are quickly worn down by their strategy, and finally just give up.

Intents shift over time. You may begin a task with the intent of getting it right, then find that you're running out of time and have to shift to getting it done. When starting a new job, you may lean more toward getting along, but over time you may come to focus more on getting appreciation.

The key points:

Understand that behaviors are sometimes driven by the intent to get it done: This isn't necessarily bad or inappropriate. In fact, it may be needed.

Know the dynamics of the intent to get it done: It causes people to focus on the task, to speed up, to assert themselves. They may become careless, treat other people as peripheral, and act aggressively.

Recognize that the intent to get it done can lead to controlling behaviors: These can express themselves as the bullying of the Tank, the lethal comments of the Sniper, or the dominating lectures of the Know-It-All. But what they all have in common is they seek to take charge of you and the situation.

"If you need to get it done, you focus on the task at hand. Any awareness of people is peripheral or unnecessary to accomplishing the task. ... You tend to speed up ..., to act ..., to assert .... You may even become careless and aggressive."

☐ Counter the behavior

☑ Understand the second intent: get it right

Getting it right is another task-focused intent that influences behavior. Have you ever sought to avoid a mistake by doing everything possible to prevent it from happening? When getting it right is your highest priority, you slow things down enough to see the details. You probably take a good, long look before leaping—if you ever leap at all. You may avoid taking any action because you feel unsure about what might happen as a result.

When the intent to get it right becomes thwarted or threatened, everything around this person begins to seem haphazard and careless. To add insult to injury, people seem to address these concerns with increasingly fuzzy terms.

When sufficient intensity is reached, the result is increasingly pessimistic and perfectionist behav-

ior. The Whiner, the No Person, and the Nothing Person all exemplify this behavior.

The Whiner. In our imperfect world, the Whiner believes that he or she is powerless to create change. Burdened and overwhelmed by all the uncertainty around what can go wrong, Whiners abandon all thought of solutions. Instead, as the feeling of hopelessness increases, they focus on any problems that can be used as evidence for their massive generalization. They begin to whine, "Nothing is right. Everything is wrong." This, of course, serves only to drive everybody else crazy—and the deteriorating situation provokes further whining.

The No Person. Unlike the Whiner, the No Person does not feel helpless in the face of things going wrong. Instead, the No Person becomes hopeless. Certain that what is wrong will never be set right, No People have no inhibition about letting others know how they feel. "Forget it, we tried that. It didn't work then, it won't work now, and you're kidding yourself if anyone tells you different. Give up and save yourself from wasted effort on a lost cause." This attitudinal black hole pulls others into the No Person's personal pit of despair.

The Nothing Person. When events fail to measure up to the standard of perfection, some people get so totally frustrated that they withdraw completely. There may be one last shout at the powers that be for failing to get it right: "Fine! Do it your way. Don't come crying to me if it doesn't work out!" From that point on they say—and do—nothing.

The key points:

Understand that behaviors are sometimes driven by the intent to get it right: Again, this isn't necessarily bad or inappropriate. In fact, it may be exactly what the situation calls for.

Know the dynamics of the intent to get it right: People concentrate on avoiding mistakes and slow down to pay more attention to all of the details. They may not take action because of concerns about the consequences. They may find fault with others for not caring enough.

Recognize that the intent to get it right can lead to perfectionist behaviors: This can express itself as the whining of the Whiner, the negativity of the No Person, or the silent withdrawal of the Nothing Person. But what they all have in common is their sureness that nothing works out positively.

"When getting it right is your highest priority, you will likely slow things down enough to see the details .... You may even refuse to take action because of a particular doubt about the consequences."

☐ Counter ~~the behavior~~

☑ Understand the third intent: get along

A third intent is to get along with other people. This is necessary if you want to create and develop relationships. When there are people with whom you want to get along, you may be less assertive as you consider their needs and interests above your own. In other words, personal desires are of lesser importance than the intent to get along with another person.

The problem is that when people who are focused on getting along with others are uncertain about how others feel about them, they tend to take reactions, comments, and facial expressions personally. *Behavior becomes increasingly geared toward gaining approval and avoiding disapproval.* The three most difficult approval-seeking behaviors are the passive Nothing Person, the wishy-washy Yes Person, and the indecisive Maybe Person.

The Nothing Person. Timid, uncomfortable, and uncertain, *get along* Nothing People excel at tongue-biting. Since they don't have anything nice to say, they don't say anything at all. At their worst, they say nothing almost all the time. This, in many ways, is the perfect strategy to avoid conflict, to avoid hurting someone else's feelings, and to keep from angering anyone. However, since a Nothing Person can't relate authentically or speak honestly, he or she doesn't really get along with anyone.

The Yes Person. Yes People attempt to get along with others by trying to please everyone. A Yes Person agrees to every request, without considering the consequences. Before long, the Yes Person has overpromised and underdelivered to such an extent that the very people he or she wanted to get along with are furious. In the rare instance where the promises are kept, the Yes Person's life is no longer his or her own, because all choices are made around other people's demands. This produces a deep-seated anxiety and much resentment in the Yes Person and can even lead to unconscious acts of sabotage.

The Maybe Person. The Maybe Person avoids disapproval by avoiding decisions. After all, the wrong choice might upset someone, and who would be blamed? The solution is to put the decision off, waffle, and hedge until someone else makes the decision—or the decision makes itself. Like all the other difficult behaviors, this behavior perpetuates the problem it's intended to solve, mainly by causing so much frustration and annoyance that the Maybe Person is locked out of meaningful relationships with others.

The key points:

Understand that behaviors are sometimes driven by the intent to get along: As we will see in subsequent chapters, establishing common ground is a good technique. But basing your actions—and your self-esteem—on your perceptions of how others see you is usually counterproductive.

Know the dynamics of the intent to get along: People tend to feel unsure about how others feel about them, so they take reactions, comments, and facial expressions personally and behave in ways that they believe will gain approval and or at least avoid disapproval.

Recognize that the intent to get along can lead to approval-seeking behaviors: This can express itself as the withdrawn Nothing Person, the agreeable Yes Person, and the indecisive Maybe Person. But what they all have in common is you really don't know where they stand.

"If getting along is your top priority ..., personal desires are less important than the intent to get along with another person."

☐ Counter the behavior

☑ Understand the fourth intent: get appreciated

This fourth intent requires a higher level of assertiveness, as well as a people focus, in order to be seen, heard, and recognized. The desire to contribute to others and *be appreciated for it* is one of the most powerful motivators. Studies show that people who love their jobs—as well as husbands and wives who are happily married—feel appreciated for who they are and what they do.

When the intent to get appreciated becomes distorted, the lack of positive feedback combines in a person's mind with the reactions, comments, and facial expressions of others and the person tends to take it personally. The intent to get appreciation intensifies in direct proportion to the lack of appreciative feedback and the problem behavior becomes *increasingly aimed at getting attention*.

The three most difficult attention-getting behaviors that result from the desire to get appreciation are the Grenade, the Sniper, and the Think-They-Know-It-All.

The Grenade. Grenades feel they don't get any appreciation or respect. When the silence becomes deafening, look out for the Grenade's grown-up temper tantrum: "Nobody around here cares! That's the problem with the world today. I don't know why I even bother!" (While the Tank uses focused fire in a single direction, based on a specific charge, the Grenade produces out-of-control explosions in any and every direction: his or her outbursts may be completely unrelated to present circumstances.) Since this desperate behavior produces negative attention and disgust, the Grenade is even more likely to blow up at the next provocation.

The Friendly Sniper. This Sniper, a variation on the unfriendly sniper who's trying to undermine your self-control, actually likes you and his or her sniping is a "fun" way of getting attention. Many people have relationships that include friendly sniping. Normally, the best defense is a good offense, because instead of offending, a return snipe is a sign of appreciation. But if the person on the receiving end doesn't give or receive appreciation in this manner, he or she may be laughing on the outside and hurting on the inside.

The Think-They-Know-It-All. The Think-They-Know-It-All is a specialist in exaggeration, half-truths, jargon, useless advice, and unsolicited opinions. Charismatic and enthusiastic, this desperate-for-attention person can persuade and mislead an entire group of naïve people into serious difficulties. If you argue with the Think-They-Know-It-Alls, they turn up the volume and dig in their heels, then refuse to back down until you look as foolish as they do.

The key points:

Understand that behaviors are sometimes driven by the intent to get appreciated: We all want to be appreciated. It's how we get there that counts.

Know the dynamics of the intent to get appreciated: People who become more concerned about receiving positive attention can take lack of affirmative feedback personally and read too much into reactions, comments, and facial expressions.

Recognize that the intent to get appreciated can lead to attention-seeking behaviors: This can express itself as the tantrums of the Grenade, the barbed jokes of the Friendly Sniper, or the boastfulness of the Think-They-Know-It-All. But what they all have in common is they force you to notice them.

"The desire to contribute to others and be appreciated for it is one of the most powerful motivational forces known."

☐ Focus on ~~behavior~~, not reasons

☑ Recognize the results of threatened intents

The four intents—get it done, get it right, get along, and get appreciated—have their time and place in our lives. The priority of those intents can shift from moment to moment. We normally balance them, for more success and less stress.

But what happens when a person's intent is not met? Let's look at each of the four intents and the results when those intents are threatened (see diagram).

- When people want to *get it done* and fear that it's not getting done, their behavior becomes more *controlling*. They try to take over and push ahead.

- When people want to *get it right* and fear that it will be done wrong, their behavior becomes more *perfectionistic*. They find every flaw and potential error.

- When people want to *get along* and fear that they will be left out, their behavior becomes more *approval* seeking. They begin sacrificing their personal needs to please others.

- When people want to *get appreciation* and fear they're failing at that intent, their behavior becomes more *attention getting*. They become difficult to ignore.

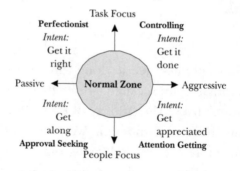

And so it begins: a person who might otherwise be inclined to act within the "normal zone" of human interaction starts drifting outside that zone, into a "gray zone" of less acceptable behavior and even into problem behavior.

The key points:

Understand that each of the four intents grows out of human nature: People are only human, after all!

Know that each intent leads to predictable kinds of behaviors: People who want to *get it done* become more *controlling*. People who want to *get it right* become more *perfectionistic*. People who want to *get along* become more *approval seeking*. People who want to *get appreciation* become more *attention getting*.

Be alert to signs that someone's behavior is going beyond the "normal zone": That's when people who are acting acceptably start to become the people you can't stand.

"Once people determine that what they want is not happening, or that what they don't want is happening, their behavior becomes more extreme and therefore less tolerable to others."

☐ Accept differences as obstacles

☑ Reduce differences

What makes some people so easy to relate to and others so difficult? We argue that conflict in a relationship occurs when the emphasis is on the *differences*, rather than on the *similarities*. Think of it as "United we stand, divided we can't stand each other."

So *reducing differences* is essential to dealing with people you can't stand. Success in communication depends on finding common ground, and then trying to redirect the interaction toward a new outcome.

Two essential communication skills will help you reduce differences: *blending* and *redirecting*. "Blending" refers to behavior by which you reduce the differences between yourself and another person. "Redirecting" is any behavior by which you use a growing rapport to change the trajectory of your interactions. These skills are not new, of course; they are part of normal human contact. In fact, you already use them, to some extent.

You can (and probably *do)* blend with people in many ways. Visually, you may blend by altering your facial expression, degree of animation, and body posture to match the other person. Verbally, blending occurs when you try to match the volume and speed of your counterpart's speech. And you blend conceptually with your words. When people feel like you've listened to them and you understand them, that's the result of blending. It's natural to blend with people whom you like or with people with whom you share an objective. Conversely, it's equally natural *not to blend* with people whom you perceive as difficult. But the failure to blend has serious consequences, because without blending, the differences between you become the basis for conflict.

Three key points:

Remember that no one cooperates with anyone who seems to be against him or her: In human relations, there's no middle ground. Unconsciously or consciously, people want to know, "Are you with me or against me?" You come across as either hot or cold in the relationship—perceived as being on common ground or as worlds apart.

Reduce the differences between yourself and the other person: You can blend by modifying your facial expression, your gestures, your posture, the volume and speed of your speech, and your words.

Blend before you redirect, whether you're listening to understand or speaking to be understood: Only after establishing some rapport with your difficult person through blending will you be able to redirect the interaction and change the trajectory toward a worthwhile outcome. In dealing with a particularly difficult person, try to recall instances in which you have successfully blended with or redirected this person in the past and try to imagine circumstances in which you might do so again.

"Conflict occurs when the emphasis is on differences. Reducing differences can turn conflict into cooperation."

☐ Make people understand you first

☑ Listen to understand

When people express themselves verbally, they generally want evidence of at least two things: they've been heard and they've been understood. A good communicator tries first to be a good listener. We advocate five steps toward good listening.

The first step toward good listening—introduced in the last lesson—is *blending*. How does someone know that you're listening and understanding? In essence, it's through the way you look and sound while they're talking. Rather than distracting a difficult person with puzzled looks, interruptions, or statements of disagreements, help him or her to fully express his or her thoughts and feelings. You do this by nodding your head in agreement, making occasional sounds of understanding. Everything about you, from body posture to voice volume, must give the impression that you hear and understand.

When your problem person begins to repeat what's already been said, it's a signal to move to step two: *backtracking*. This involves repeating back some of the actual words that another person is using, sending a clear signal that you're listening and that you think what the other person is saying is important. Translating or rephrasing what they have said is counterproductive and may create the impression that you haven't understood what's been said.

Having heard what the difficult person has to say, the next step is *clarifying*. At this point, you start to gather information about the meaning of what is being communicated. Ask some open-ended questions, which will allow you to figure out why the person is being difficult and what intent he or she is hoping to satisfy with that behavior.

It isn't always possible to understand why someone is upset. Emotions so cloud the reasoning capabilities of many people that their intelligence effectively becomes disconnected from their feelings. While it's virtually impossible to reason with an emotional person, it's still possible to look and sound like you understand, backtrack what you've heard, and then become curious enough to ask questions.

The fourth step is to *summarize* what you've heard. This allows you to make sure that both you and your difficult person are on the same page. When you do this, two things happen. First, if you've missed something, he or she can fill in the details. Second, you've demonstrated, yet again, that you're making a serious effort to fully understand. This increases the likelihood of gaining cooperation from that person down the line.

Having listened carefully, you've now arrived at a crucial juncture. But before you move on, *confirm* with the person that he or she feels satisfied that his or her problem has been fully voiced. Ask if he or she feels understood. Ask if there's anything else that needs to be put on the table.

When enough sincere listening, questioning, caring, and remembering are brought together, understanding is usually achieved and a difficult person becomes less difficult and more cooperative.

The key points:

Listen first, listen well: You aren't likely to be heard (or understood) until the person has said what he or she has to say.

Learn and practice the five steps to good listening: Blend, backtrack, clarify, summarize, and confirm.

Make sure the other person knows you've heard and understood: You must establish this fact before you attempt to get him or her to hear and understand you.

"When two or more people want to be heard and no one is willing to listen, an argument is inevitable. Listen and understand first, and you unlock the doors to people's minds."

☐ Just deal with behaviors

☑ Reach a deeper understanding

We've discussed listening as a method for increasing trust, cooperation, and understanding. Yet sometimes the most important and useful aspects of communication are hidden—not just from the listener, but also from the speaker. When you identify the elements driving the difficult person, you reach a deeper understanding of that person's needs and intent.

Identifying the intent is an important first step to understanding your difficult person. You can apply the blending strategy to the four intents to increase cooperation and decrease misunderstanding.

For example:

- If you're dealing with someone whose top priority appears to be to *get it done*, your communications with him or her should be brief and to the point.

45

- If you're dealing with someone whose top priority appears to be to *get it right*, you should pay great attention to the details in your communications.

- If you're dealing with someone whose top priority appears to be to *get along* with you, use considerate communications to demonstrate your interest in him or her.

- If you're dealing with someone whose top priority appears to be to *get appreciated*, recognize his or her contributions with words of enthusiastic appreciation.

In other words, it's crucial to ask yourself which intent lies behind a person's behavior or communication. Here's a surprise: *even if you're not totally sure what the key intent is, make the likely choice and act appropriately*. Because these intents are within you, in most cases your intuition will be right and you'll get a good response and increase rapport. And if it is not, then simply try something different.

Another way to reach a deeper understanding of your problem person is to *identify the criteria that are important to them*. Criteria are the filters on our points of view—the standards by which we measure ideas and experiences to determine if they're good or bad. Criteria become especially important when differing ideas or points of view are being discussed. Any time you identify criteria in a discussion, you generate more flexibility and cooperation.

Whenever a discussion starts to degenerate into conflict, try to ascertain the reasons why people are for or against something. Then look for an idea or solution to the problem that blends those criteria together. That's another way to turn conflict into cooperation.

The key points:

Identify and act on intents: If, for example, someone appears to need your appreciation, make your appreciation clear.

Act on intent even when you're not sure of intent: Because these intents are within you, let your intuition guide you. And if what you're doing isn't working, then simply do something else.

Use criteria to reach a deeper understanding: What are the filters that your difficult person is using? How can you use your understanding of those filters to create new options?

"This ... is about ... the kind of understanding that will help you communicate effectively, prevent future conflict, and resolve current conflict before it gets out of hand ..., the kind of understanding that results when you ... closely examine the difficult behavior until you can see the motive behind it."

☐ ~~Just make your point~~

☑ **Speak to be understood**

We've advocated effective listening as the best way to increase trust, cooperation, and understanding—and as a prerequisite for effective communication back to your difficult person. When you express yourself, it's important to do so in ways that produce positive effects. The signals, symbols, and suggestions that constitute our communication output provide a profound opportunity to influence relationships for the better. Here are six effective techniques.

Monitor your tone of voice. Your tone sends people either a positive or a negative message. Even when you choose your words well, if your tone of voice is hurried, hostile, or defensive, people may hear something very different from what you intended.

Mixed messages, caused by voice tones that don't match spoken words, cause miscommunications. If you hear yourself sending a mixed message, call attention to it and explain what you're really saying: "I know I sound angry, but that is because this issue is so important to me."

State your key intent. Articulating your key intent lets people know where you're coming from. When your key intent is implied rather than stated clearly, misunderstanding can result. Telling people why you're telling them something before you actually tell them is a simple way to direct attention where you want it to go.

Tactfully interrupt. There are occasions when it is necessary to interrupt a difficult person. If someone is yelling at you, dominating a meeting, or complaining in endless cycles of negativity, an interruption may be an elegant solution. Done carefully, it can also be tactful.

A tactful interruption is done without anger, without blame, and without fear. Just say the difficult person's name over and over, in a matter-of-fact way, until you get his or her attention. These repetitions create an irresistible force that so distracts Tanks, Know-It-Alls, Grenades, or Whiners that they must stop talking to find out what you want.

Tell your truth. Honesty can be effective, no matter what difficult behavior a person engages in, if you're honest in a way that builds someone up rather than tears him or her down. Remember to tell the person why you are telling your truth before you actually tell it. State your positive intent and why you think it's in the person's interest to hear what you have to say. Be sure to point out that it's *your opinion*. Then be specific about the problem behavior, show how the behavior defeats his or her intent, and suggest new behaviors to replace the old ones.

Stay flexible. If your problem person becomes defensive, be willing to temporarily drop what you're saying to focus on his or her reaction. Do your best to fully understand any objections by backtracking, clarifying, summarizing, and confirming. This may seem time-consuming, but overall, it takes less energy than an adversarial conversation that goes nowhere.

The key points:

Once you have listened well, move on to effective speaking: One grows naturally out of the other.

Learn and practice the five techniques of speaking to be understood: Yes, effective speaking is harder and often takes longer—in the short run. But it's the best way to better outcomes in the long run.

Remember that "communicate" has the same origins as "common": To communicate is to establish a common understanding.

"What you say to people can produce defensiveness or trust, increase resistance or cooperation, promote conflict or understanding."

☐ Don't expect too much of people

☑Project and expect the best

The difficult behavior of problem people is often reinforced, and even escalated, by thoughtless and/or negative reactions from people around them. So if you want to have a positive influence, thoughtful responses are required.

It's in your interest to give difficult people the benefit of the doubt. It's also in your interest to help them break their reliance on negative behaviors and reinforce more constructive behaviors. If you do this habitually, a difficult person may come to see you as an ally rather than an enemy and be all the more ready to fulfill your positive expectations.

The power of expectations can't be underestimated. We call this phenomenon *Pygmalion Power*. If you tell people you have high expectations of them, they will not deny it. They will in fact take a step in that direction. But conversely, if you let it be known that you have low expectations, these will most likely be fulfilled, as well.

When your problem person is engaging in negative behavior, you may be tempted to say, "That's the problem with you. You always …." To use Pygmalion Power effectively, learn to say, "That's not like you! You're capable of …" and then describe how you want the person to be, as if he or she already were. And whenever your difficult person behaves well, reinforce the behavior by learning to say, "That's one of the things I like about you. You're always …" and then say what the person has done successfully so he or she will do it again.

Pygmalion Power is not the easiest technique to employ when someone is acting badly. You may have to spend some time mentally rehearsing it before you're able to talk this way with ease. You may have to force yourself to hope that the person can change, when all evidence is to the contrary. Yet, we have no doubt that you can surprise yourself delightfully with your power to bring out the best in people at their worst.

The key points:

***Understand and embrace* Pygmalion Power:** Human nature is what it is. When you tell people that they're doing something wrong, they're very likely to get defensive. You can minimize that reaction by giving them the benefit of the doubt and expecting the best. Sometimes you get it!

Appreciate criticism: This is nothing more than the flip side of Pygmalion Power. If you tend to get defensive to criticism, perhaps you've noticed that it usually makes things worse. The implication is that your defenses are an admission of guilt, and anything you say may be used against you. Here's a simple way to rapidly shut down criticism without either internalizing it or fighting against it: verbally appreciate it. A simple "thanks for the feedback" may be all that it takes, and it's over. Alternatively, you can listen effectively, helping the critical person to be specific until you learn something useful, he or she learns it isn't about you, or he or she loses interest in criticizing you.

"It's a fact that people rise or fall to the level of your expectations and projections. Use projection strategies to motivate your problem people to change themselves."

☑ Bring out the best in the Tank

When you're under attack by the Tank, you've been targeted as part of the problem. The aggressive behavior is meant to either shove you back on course or eliminate the obstacle that you represent. Your goal must be to command respect, because Tanks simply don't attack people they respect. Aggressive people require assertive reactions. Here's a five-step action plan that will send a clear signal that you are strong and capable.

Hold your ground. Stay put. Don't change your position and don't go on either the offensive or the defensive. Wait until the attack is over, then tell the Tank what you're going to do about it (even if it means walking away)—and do it. Other times, you may need to proceed to the next step.

Interrupt the attack. Say the person's name over and over until you have his or her full attention.

Once you've begun this step, don't back off. Aggressive people *like* assertive people who stand up for themselves, as long as this isn't perceived as an attack. Keep your voice volume at 75% of the Tank's volume. Then he or she will perceive you as assertive but not aggressive.

Backtrack. Now that you have the Tank's attention, backtrack the main accusation. This sets a good example of listening with respect and conveys that you've heard him or her. A Tank has a short attention span. Two sentences will do. He or she will go back to venting. Wait a few seconds, then interrupt again and backtrack again.

Aim for the bottom line and fire! Redirect the conversation to the bottom line—the Tank's if he or she is right, yours if he or she is wrong. The Tank wants to get it done, and your best chance of ending the attack is to blend with his or her intent. The bottom line varies with your situation, but can usually be stated in about two sentences. Keep it short and sweet: the attention span of a Tank is extremely short. Try to establish that you and he or she are on the same side: e.g., "We both want what's best on this project." Or respond with a problem: e.g., "That's terrible, I'm here to help you and we're going to do something about it!" A take-charge attitude will definitely blend with a Tank. If you're not on the same side, just tell it like it is: e.g., "I'll discuss this with you when you're ready to communicate in a reasonable manner."

Peace with honor. Never close the door in the Tank's face. When you leave the door open, the Tank has the opportunity to back off and probably will take it. You can let him or her have the last word ... but you decide where and when this happens: e.g., "When you're ready to talk to me with respect, I'm willing to hear what you have to say."

There are three typical emotional responses to an attacking Tank. They're all natural—and all futile. So adjust your attitude:

Don't counterattack! Avoid engaging with the Tank. You may win the battle, but you could still lose the war if the Tank decides to build an alliance against you.

Don't defend, explain, or justify: The Tank has no interest in your explanations and defensive behavior is likely to further antagonize the Tank.

Don't shut down: Out of fear or to avoid conflict, you may be tempted to withdraw. But fear is a surefire sign to the Tank that the attack was justified and may inspire him or her to return for more.

"The Tank is confrontational, pointed, and angry, the ultimate in pushy and aggressive behavior."

☑ Bring out the best in the Sniper

When events don't go as planned or are obstructed by others, a *get it done* person may try to eliminate the opposition through sniping. Your goal when dealing with the Sniper is to bring him or her out of hiding. Since the Sniper's limited power is derived from covert operations, rather than overt, once you've exposed a Sniping position, that position becomes useless.

Stop, look, backtrack. Since your goal is to bring the Sniper out of hiding, you must first zero in on his or her hiding place. If it seems that someone is taking shots at you, stop!—even in the middle of a sentence. Interrupting yourself brings attention to the Sniper, effectively blowing his or her cover. Look directly into the person's eyes for a moment, and then calmly backtrack his or her remark.

Use searchlight questions. Now it's time to turn on the searchlight, asking a question to draw the Sniper out and expose his or her behavior. The two best questions are based on intent and relevancy: "When you say that (backtrack), what are you really trying to say?" and "What does that (backtrack) have to do with this?" The key to asking a searchlight question is to keep your tone neutral and maintain a neutral (read "innocent") look on your face.

Use Tank strategy if necessary. If a Sniper becomes a Tank, you may have actually improved the situation; at least now you know what the problem is! Use the strategy recommended for dealing with the Tank not only to command respect from the Sniper, but also from those who have witnessed the attack.

Go on a grievance patrol. If you suspect that someone is holding a grudge against you, but you're not certain, see what you can scout out. If you find evidence that someone is harboring a grudge, you may want to clear the air. If you're successful in bringing the grudge to the surface, listen carefully to all that your Sniper has to say. Once you fully understand the grievance, let your problem person know that you understand and express appreciation for his or her candid description of the problem.

Suggest a civil future. Whether in private or public, finish the interaction by suggesting an alternative behavior for the future. At the end of any encounter with the Sniper, it's important to let him or her know that your preference in the future is open and friendly communication. So ...

Don't overreact: Reacting strongly to the Sniper may encourage him or her to dish out more of the same. The best attitude to develop is one of amused curiosity. Try not to take it personally; instead, focus on the Sniper, rather than yourself.

Distinguish between friendly Snipers and malicious Snipers: Friendly Sniping has its origins in the intent to get appreciated, the need for attention. Malicious Sniping, on the other hand, originates in the intent to get it done and fulfills the need for control by seeking to undermine the control of others.

For the friendly Sniper, try reframing: Take the remark as a sign of affection or a behavioral quirk. If you can't laugh at it, you can at least learn to laugh it off. Or just let the Sniper know you don't respond well to teasing or put-down humor. Since the person likes you, he or she may change his or her behavior around you. And when that happens, reinforce it by appreciating the person for the change.

"Whether through rude comments, biting sarcasm, or a well-timed roll of the eyes, making you look foolish is the Sniper's specialty."

☑ Bring out the best in the Know-It-All

Know-It-Alls are knowledgeable and extremely competent people, highly assertive and outspoken in their viewpoints. Their intent is to get it done in the way that they have determined is best, so they can be very controlling, with a low tolerance for correction and contradiction. Know-It-Alls perceive new ideas as challenges to their authority and knowledge and will rise to those challenges. They will do anything to avoid humiliation.

Your goal with the Know-It-All is to open his or her mind to new information and ideas. But as we've seen, this isn't easy(!). With Know-It-Alls, it's next to impossible to get your two cents in.

Be prepared and know your stuff. If there are any flaws in your thinking, Know-It-All radar will pick up on those shortcomings and use them to discredit

65

your whole idea. In order to get a Know-It-All to consider your alternative, you must clearly think through your information beforehand and be ready to present it clearly and concisely.

Backtrack respectfully. Be forewarned: you'll have to do more backtracking with the Know-It-All than with any other difficult person. They must feel that you have thoroughly understood the brilliance of their point of view before you'll be able to redirect them to another point of view.

It's not enough to simply backtrack; your whole demeanor must be one of respect and sincerity. You want to look and sound like the Know-It-All's view is in fact the correct one.

Blend with their doubts and desires. If the Know-It-All really believes in an idea, it is because of specific criteria that make that idea important to him or her. You will find it helpful to blend with those criteria, if you know them, by acknowledging them before you present your idea. Then show how your idea takes those factors into account.

Present your views indirectly. When the time has come to redirect the Know-It-All to your position, use softening words like "maybe," "perhaps," and "bear with me a moment" to sound hypothetical and indirect, rather than determined or challenging. Try questions rather than statements and "we" rather than "I."

Turn them into mentors. By letting the Know-It-All know that you recognize an expert and are willing to learn, you become less of a threat. This way, the Know-It-All spends more time *in*structing you than *ob*structing you. It is entirely possible that, with time, the Know-It-All may be more willing to listen to you, as well.

Adjust your attitude:

Don't use the Know-It-All's weapons: Resist the temptation of becoming a Know-It-All yourself. It will only serve to entrench the Know-It-All more firmly.

Don't resent the Know-It-All: It's not in the Know-It-All's nature to get a second opinion. Resentments will only lead to an argument, which is pointless.

Don't force your ideas on the Know-It-All: Train yourself to be flexible, patient, and very clever about how you present your ideas.

"Seldom in doubt, the Know-It-All has a low tolerance for correction and contradiction. If something goes wrong, however, the Know-It-All will speak with the same authority about who's to blame—you!"

☑ Bring out the best in the Think-They-Know-It-All

People who behave like Think-They-Know-It-Alls are driven by the need to get appreciation. When they feel slighted in any way, they're likely to try harder than ever to attract attention. Think-They-Know-It-Alls push their way into conversations where they may not be wanted.

Your goal when dealing with Think-They-Know-It-Alls is to catch them in their act and give their bad ideas the hook. You'll be most successful if you can avoid putting the Think-They-Know-It-All on the defensive. Here's an action plan for bringing out the best in Think-They-Know-It-Alls.

Give them a little attention. There are two ways to give a Think-They-Know-It-All attention. The first is to backtrack on his or her comments with enthusiasm. This lets the person know that you're paying attention (and it puts these types on the receiving end of their own foolishness). The second way is to acknowledge the person's positive intent, without wasting your time on his or her information: you're giving positive attention without necessarily agreeing with his or her remarks.

Clarify for specifics. If the person doesn't know what he or she is talking about and you do, this should be easy. Ask some revealing questions about the specifics of his or her information. Since Think-They-Know-It-Alls speak in huge generalizations, pay special attention to words like "everybody" and "always."

Tell it like it is. Carefully redirect the conversation back to reality. Use "I" language to keep your remarks as nonthreatening as possible. To add irrefutable evidence, you can document your facts as you go.

Give them a break. At this point, it has become clear that the Think-They-Know-It-All doesn't know what he or she is talking about and that you do. Resist the temptation to embarrass the person. Instead, give him or her a way out, minimizing the chance that the Think-They-Know-It-All will go on the defensive. Think-They-Know-It-Alls are not as attached to their ideas as Know-It-Alls. If you give them a way to go along with you, chances are they'll be ready to jump on your bandwagon.

Break the cycle. Once people believe someone is just a Think-They-Know-It-All, they may stop giving that person any recognition at all, even when he or she deserves it. But that increases the Think-They-Know-It-All's need for appreciation, so he or she engages in that behavior even more. "Break the cycle" means be ready to give credit where credit is due. Notice what this problem person is doing right and praise him or her for it. For some people, this attention will be all that's necessary to get the problem behavior to subside. With others, use a gentle confrontation to tell them the truth about the consequences of their negative behavior.

Adjust your attitude:

Don't burst their bubble: When you challenge Think-They-Know-It-Alls directly, their only way out is to counterattack with ever grander claims. And their conviction could sway others who don't know any better.

Don't be too quick to judge: We've all defended ideas that we didn't necessarily believe to be true.

"Think-They-Know-It-Alls can't fool all of the people all of the time, but they can fool some of the people enough of the time and enough of the people all of the time—all for the sake of getting some attention."

☑ Bring out the best in the Grenade

When a person's efforts to get appreciation are thwarted by another's indifference, he or she may explode in a thinly disguised demand for attention. Losing emotional control is a defense strategy against the feeling of unimportance—a strategy frequently employed by the Grenade.

If, as an adult in a group, you've ever lost control of yourself, you know how humiliating this can be. Grenades hate themselves for their behavior—but this self-hatred often becomes the timing device that provokes the next explosion. This volatile cycle can continue unchecked, meaning that an ounce of prevention can be worth far more than a pound of cure! Here are the five steps to bringing out the best in the Grenade.

Get the Grenade's attention. This is the one time you may have to be louder than your problem person … but don't let it seem aggressive. Call his or her name loudly, but in a tone of voice that's interested rather than angry.

Aim for the heart. Show your genuine concern by telling your problem person what he or she needs to hear. By listening closely, you can determine the cause of the explosion, then backtrack while assuring the person of your concern. When you hit the heart, you'll be surprised at how quickly the Grenade cools down.

Reduce intensity. When you see the Grenade responding, begin to reduce your voice volume and intensity. You can talk the person down from his or her peak of explosion to a normal level of communication by reducing the intensity level of your own communications.

Take time off for bad behavior. There's no point in trying to have a reasonable conversation with your problem person while the adrenaline is still coursing. So take a little time out and let things cool the rest of the way down. Then ask to get back together to work things out.

Avoid setting off the Grenade. This step addresses the long-term relationship and is, therefore, the most important in dealing with your problem person. Try to figure out what pulls the pin on your Grenade … and then don't pull it! If you discover that the pin-puller is someone else in the office, training in interpersonal communication and conflict resolution might be helpful.

Adjust your attitude:

Release your anger: Adding your anger to an already volatile situation will simply be pouring gas on a raging fire.

Learn to look at the Grenade in a different way: Sometimes it can help to imagine the tantrum thrower as a two-year-old in diapers. Adjusting your perception of the Grenade will give you some much needed distance on the situation.

Listen to the Grenade: Whatever the cause of the explosions, if you're willing to invest a little time in actively listening to the problems the Grenade faces, you will slowly be able to reduce the frequency and intensity of the explosions.

"After a brief period of calm, the Grenade explodes into unfocused ranting and raving about things that have nothing to do with the present circumstances."

☑ Bring out the best in the Yes Person

Yes People have a strong people focus and a weak task focus. They are extremely disorganized and frequently overcommit themselves as they try to run their lives based on the desires of other people. Sometimes they don't know how to follow through on something they've agreed to do; more often than not, they don't think about the consequences of what they're agreeing to do.

Yes People feel terrible when they can't deliver something they've promised. Yet they rarely feel responsible, because they can always find circumstances beyond their control that have caused the trouble.

Your goal with the Yes Person is to get commitments you can count on. Here are five steps to bringing out the best in the Yes Person.

Make it safe to be honest. Through nonverbal blending and verbal reassurance, make sure your communication environment is safe, so that you and your Yes Person can honestly examine whether he or she will keep promises. As the person becomes more comfortable with you, his or her true thoughts and feelings will surface more easily.

Talk honestly. If you think the Yes Person is angry or resentful about something or believes the excuses he or she is spinning, talk it out. Hear the person out without contradicting, jumping to conclusions, or taking offense. Acknowledge him or her for being honest.

Help them learn to plan. Once you've listened to your Yes Person's point of view, it will be obvious to you why the person can't deliver on his or her commitments. This is the time to create a learning opportunity. Teaching your Yes Person simple task-management skills is a better use of your energy than getting upset at the person when he or she can't deliver!

Ensure commitment. Thank your Yes Person for communicating openly with you and ask how he or she will approach the situation differently next time.

In future projects, make sure the Yes Person is committed at the beginning. Have him or her summarize the project to demonstrate an understanding of what's involved. Write the commitment down. You may even come up with memorable deadlines to ensure that the timeframe will stick. Finally, be sure to describe the negative consequences should your Yes Person fail to deliver.

Strengthen the relationship. Look at every interaction as a chance to strengthen the relationship. Make an event out of every completed commitment and see mistakes and broken promises as an opportunity to help the Yes Person develop his or her skills.

Adjust your attitude:

Don't place blame: Blaming the Yes Person will simply make him or her ashamed, the behavior will continue as the person promises you anything he or she thinks will placate you.

Be patient: Recognize that your Yes Person is lacking organizational skills and is unable to recognize or fix this without help. Once you've helped the Yes Person develop task skills, his or her helpful nature will make that person the best teammate you could hope for.

Help with task management: Ask the Yes Person to explain the basics of the project, the tasks involved, and any negative consequences if he or she doesn't meet the commitment. Then, help him or her plan toward the deadlines, to establish a timeframe.

"To please people and avoid confrontations, Yes People say 'Yes' without thinking things through. They react to the latest demands on their time by forgetting prior commitments and overcommit until they have no time for themselves. Then they become resentful."

☑ Bring out the best in the Maybe Person

Decisive people know that every decision has a downside and an upside and are able to weigh these possibilities as they make the best decision possible. Maybe People, by contrast, are unable to make decisions, especially when the consequences of their decisions could affect other people in a way that might lose them approval. So they put off the difficult decision, hoping that a better choice will come up. Unfortunately, with most decisions there comes a point when it's too late to choose: the decision just happens.

Maybe People have plenty of reasons for not getting help; they don't want to bother or upset anyone and they don't want to be the cause of anything going wrong. Your goal when dealing with a Maybe

Person is to give him or her a strategy for making decisions and the motivation to use it. Here are five steps to bring out the best in your Maybe Person.

Establish a comfort zone. When you're dealing with people in the *get along* quadrant, your best bet is to develop a comfort zone around the decision-making process. Take your time. Reassure the Maybe Person that you believe relationships are improved by open communication.

Surface conflicts and clarify options. Patiently explore, from the Maybe Person's point of view, all of the options and obstacles involved in the decision. Listen for words of hesitation like "probably," "that could be," and "I think so" as signals to explore more deeply. If the person is worried about how you will feel should he or she decide something, provide reassurance that you will be fine and it won't adversely affect your relationship.

Use a decision-making process. If you have a process that works well for you, teach it to your problem person. It could be as simple as listing with him or her all the pluses and minuses of each of the possibilities. Seeing these in a concrete form may make the strongest choice more obvious.

Reassure and follow through. Once the decision has been made, reassure the Maybe Person that there are no perfect decisions and that his or her decision is a good one. Then *stay in touch* until the decision is implemented.

Strengthen the relationship. Take a few moments from time to time to listen to the Maybe Person's concerns and help him or her learn the decision-making process whenever the opportunity arises. With patient investment, the Maybe Person may become one of your most dependable decision makers.

Adjust your attitude:

Don't push the Maybe Person: Irritation, impatience, or anger will simply make the decision that much more difficult.

Be patient: If your Maybe Person feels pressured, he or she won't be able to relax and think clearly.

Stay calm: Intensity or intimidation will drive Maybe People deeper into their wishy-washy behavior. Even if you can force a decision, they will probably change their minds as soon as they're pressured by someone with a different agenda.

"In a moment of decision, the Maybe Person procrastinates in the hope that a better choice will present itself. Sadly, with most decisions, there comes a point when it is too little, too late, and the decision makes itself."

☑ Bring out the best in the Nothing Person

Nothing People are passive, but can be task-focused or people-focused depending on their intent—*get it right* or *get along*. When the intent to *get along* is threatened, shy people tend to withdraw and become ever more passive. When get it right Nothing People see their quest for perfection thwarted, they get frustrated and withdraw, convinced that nothing will change the situation, no matter what they say or do.

Although Nothing People seem to withdraw from conflict, inside they can be boiling cauldrons of hostility. Silence can be their form of aggression. Your goal with a Nothing Person is to break this silence and persuade him or her to talk. Here is a surefire five-step process to break your Nothing Person's silence.

Plan enough time. Dealing successfully with a Nothing Person may take a long time. If you're tense because of time constraints, you may be too intense to draw him or her out. The more intense you get, the deeper the Nothing Person withdraws into nothing. So pick the time and place for approaching your Nothing Person so that you have the time it takes.

Ask open-ended questions expectantly. The best question for a Nothing Person is one that can't be answered with a yes, a no, or a grunt. Ask questions that begin with a "Who," "What," "When," "Where," or "How" to open up topics for discussion. Make sure that your non-verbal communication is also asking for a response. You must look and sound like you're about to get an answer. We call this the "expectant look"—and it *works*.

Lighten it up. When nothing else is working, a little humor can go a long way. Making absurd, exaggerated, and impossible guesses as to the cause of the silence has cracked the armor of some of the most intransigent Nothing People.

Guess. If your Nothing Person still isn't responding, try putting yourself in his or her shoes and thinking back over the course of events as to what that person might be feeling. Start talking out loud, rattling off possibilities whether they seem plausible or far out. It doesn't matter. If you can hit on or near the reason for the silence, the person will figure the jig is up and he or she might as well start talking. If you don't come close, the Nothing Person may figure you don't have a clue and feel compelled to tell you what is going on.

Show the future. Sometimes the only way to get Nothing People talking is to take them out of the moment and show them the consequences of their continued silence. Don't make idle threats, but be clear about how their behavior could damage the project or your relationship.

Adjust your attitude:

Slow down: The biggest challenge with a Nothing Person is to find the time to deal with him or her. To get something from a Nothing Person, you must be calm and relaxed.

Understand the intent: Nothing People can be task-focused, if their intent is to get it right, or people-focused, if their intent is to get along. Determine what matters.

Avoid getting angry: Your Nothing Person is trying to avoid conflict and disapproval. Getting angry will simply push a Nothing Person deeper into his or her nothingness.

"No verbal feedback, no nonverbal feedback. Nothing. What else could you expect from ... the Nothing Person?"

☑ Bring out the best in the No Person

The No Person is task-focused, motivated by the intent to get it right by avoiding mistakes. Perfection is his or her standard: when shortcomings get in the way, the No Person despairs and finds negatives in everyone and everything.

When dealing with a No Person, your task is to move from fault finding toward problem solving. It may be impossible to stop the flood of negativity completely, but you may be able to turn the tide. Here are five steps to dealing successfully with a No Person.

Go with the flow. The *worst thing* you can do with No People is to try to convince them that things aren't as bad as they think they are. The first step in dealing with No People is to allow them to be as negative as they want to be.

Use them as a resource. No People can serve two valuable purposes in your life. First, they can be your personal character builders. If you want to build strength, you lift heavy weights. If you want to build a positive attitude, spend some time being positive with a No Person.

No People can also serve as an early warning system. Amid the negativity, there are often grains of truth. The No Person is sometimes aware of substantial problems that others have overlooked. We know of one company that has a No Person on its executive staff. By running every new plan by her, they often find flaws that might otherwise have been overlooked.

Leave the door open. No People tend to operate in a different time reality from other people. Any effort to rush them may actually slow them down. The wisest course of action with No People is to give them time to think, and leave the door open so that they can come back in when they're ready.

Go for the polarity response. Sometimes, you can turn the tables on your No Person by suggesting the negative alternatives before he or she does. In such cases, No People may respond positively—either because they're convinced by your approach that you're dealing with the problem realistically or because they're so incurably negative that they want to prove you wrong even if they agree with you.

Acknowledge their good intent. Assume and project good intent onto negative behavior, like

"Thanks for pointing out problems so we can all come up with solutions" or "I appreciate that you want this to be right." Through Pygmalion Power, the No Person may come to believe it. This can lead the person to use his or her analytical perfectionism in a more constructive—and less difficult—way.

Adjust your attitude:

Maintain your perspective: There's usually some bad history involved when people behave negatively. You don't need to know what the circumstances are, but try to keep the No Person's actions in perspective.

Be patient: It may sometimes appear that changes take place at a snail's pace. But if you are patient, there are few things as gratifying as people conquering their negative behavior.

Appreciate the No Person: He or she may bring up points worth considering, if you're wise enough to sort through the negativity. Just because the No Person goes to extremes doesn't mean that he or she is wrong.

"More deadly to morale than a speeding bullet, more powerful than hope, able to defeat big ideas with a single syllable. Disguised as a mild-mannered normal person, the No Person fights a never-ending battle for futility, hopelessness, and despair."

☑ Bring out the best in the Whiner

While some complaining can be therapeutic for the complainer, and some can even be helpful to the listener, lots of complaining is simply wallowing. This is the Whiner's specialty. The Whiner's complaints have little to do with stress relief and are rarely helpful. Whiners are cousins to the No People, in the sense that their actions also emerge from the intent to get it right. But while they have a sense that things should be different, they have no idea how this should happen. So instead of taking action, they whine.

Your goal with Whiners is to form a problem-solving alliance. (And if this doesn't work, your revised goal is to get them to go away!) The best thing you can do for people who feel helpless when they encounter difficulty is to *diminish their helplessness*, by working with them to identify solutions.

Here are five action steps to work successfully with a Whiner.

Listen for the main points. Listening to a Whiner complain is probably the last thing you want to do. But it's a crucial first step. You may even want to take notes. This proves to the Whiner that you're listening and it will ensure that you recognize the complaint if the Whiner tries to recycle it.

Interrupt and get specific. Take command of the conversation and ask clarification questions to get the specifics of the problem. If your Whiner isn't able to be specific, suggest that he or she go out and gather more information.

Shift the focus to solutions. Because Whiners often complain in vague generalizations, they don't usually look at problems long enough to start thinking about solutions. Asking them what they want can start to move their minds in an entirely new direction.

Show them the future. When people feel helpless, it's constructive to give them something to look forward to. Offer to set up a meeting with the person they're complaining about or simply set a time to discuss the problem further. You may find it helpful to suggest that they come back to you with possible solutions within a specific time frame.

Draw the line. If the previous steps haven't produced a real change, it may become necessary to draw the line. If your Whiner begins the cycle of complaints again, shut him or her down. Make it clear that talking about problems without solutions isn't a good use of your time … or anyone's.

Adjust your attitude:

Don't agree or disagree with Whiners: If you agree, it simply encourages them to keep whining. If you disagree, they may feel compelled to repeat their problems.

Don't try to solve Whiners' problems: You won't be able to solve their problems for them; you'll need their participation.

Don't ask Whiners why they're complaining: They'll simply see this as an invitation to start over from the beginning.

"Whiners feel helpless and overwhelmed by an unfair world. Their standard is perfection, and no one and nothing measures up to it. But misery loves company, so they bring their problems to you. Offering solutions makes you bad company, so their whining escalates."

☐ ~~Wait until there's a problem~~

☑ Take the first three action steps

The communication lessons in this book are not intended to be a quick fix, but a path to long-term solutions for problems in human relationships. The longer it takes for a problem to develop, the more time and energy you must invest in turning things around. As you begin to apply these attitudes and strategies, chances are that you will have some easy successes ... and some unsuccessful efforts. More important than "winning" or "losing," though, is having more choices, opportunities, and alternatives to suffering. You can now empower yourself to be the cause of what happens next, rather than the victim of what others have done.

Difficult people are a part of every person's life. They've been here since the beginning of time—

running away, blaming, withdrawing. But with commitment and perseverance, each of us can do our part to reduce misunderstandings and eliminate the conflicts that plague the earth. And without becoming too grandiose, we think it's fair to say that the future of humanity depends on each of us *learning how to stand each other*, in spite of our differences.

Though you can't directly change anyone else, your flexibility and knowledge can help people to change themselves. So the next time you're dealing with someone you can't stand, remember this: Life is not a test, it's an actual emergency. Good luck!

Here are a few simple action steps you can take immediately:

Resolve to become an effective communicator: Make it your goal to become an effective communicator; take advantage of all available opportunities to practice and perfect these techniques. Pay attention! Whether you're watching a movie or attending a meeting, you'll find lots of examples of people using or failing to use the skills and strategies in this book.

Find a communication partner: Team up with communication partners who are as eager to learn as you are. Share resources (like this book) with your partners so that you'll have a common language in your discussions. Meet once a week to discuss what you've observed, learned, and tried during the preceding week. More than any other action you can take, regular meetings with communication partners can remind you to pay attention, while keeping you focused on developing and improving your skill.

Count your blessings! If you have the luxury of reading this book, you're already better off than perhaps 80% of the earth's population. You probably have a roof over your head, sufficient food, people you care about, and some who care about you. Life is difficult enough without filling yourself with negativity and wasting your life force on worry and stress. If you remember to count your blessings today and everyday, then you'll have the strength and focus to enjoy the challenges presented by difficult people.

"While you can't change difficult people, you can communicate with them in such a way that they change themselves. It's a matter of knowing how to get through to them when they're behaving badly."

"If you work with people who are difficult, there is both good news and bad news. The bad news is you work with them. The good news is you have time to study them, understand the patterns of their behavior, and plan your strategic response."

"Think of dealing with problem people like going to the gym. They are giving you a workout of your communication muscles! Although you may not always get the result you want, the strength you build from the effort may be exactly what you need to preserve some other relationship that truly matters to you."

"What is the secret to communication effectiveness with difficult people? Flexibility. Flexibility means having more than one option. If what you're doing isn't working, do something else, or do something differently. Anything you do differently increases the likelihood of your success."

Other Titles in the McGraw-Hill Professional Education Series

How to Manage Performance: 24 Lessons for Improving Performance

by Robert Bacal (0-07-143531-X)

Dealing with Difficult People: 24 Lessons for Bringing Out the Best in Everyone

by Dr. Rick Brinkman and Dr. Rick Kirschner
(0-07-141641-2)

How to Be a Great Coach: 24 Lessons for Turning on the Productivity of Every Employee

by Marshall J. Cook (0-07-143529-8)

Making Teams Work: 24 Lessons for Working Together Successfully

by Michael Maginn (0-07-143530-1)

Why Customers Don't Do What You Want Them to Do: 24 Solutions to Overcoming Common Selling Problems

by Ferdinand Fournies (0-07-141750-8)

The Sales Success Handbook: 20 Lessons to Open and Close Sales Now

by Linda Richardson (0-07-141636-6)

About the Authors

Dr. Rick Kirschner and Dr. Rick Brinkman are world-renowned professional speakers and trainers. They are the coauthors of the bestselling audio- and video-tape series *How to Deal with Difficult People* and have authored six other audio and video training programs. Their book *Dealing with People You Can't Stand* is an international bestseller, now available in a revised second edition with translations in 15 languages. They wrote the entertaining and practical sequel *Dealing with Relatives: Your Guide to Successful Family Relationships* and they coauthored the book *Life by Design, Making Wise Choices in a Mixed Up World*. They now present their entertaining keynote speeches and training programs worldwide. Their client portfolio includes AT&T, Hewlett-Packard, the Inc. 500 Conference, Young Presidents Organization, the U.S. Army, and hundreds of other corporations, government agencies, medical conferences, educational groups, and professional associations.

For information about Dr. Kirschner's keynotes and seminars, visit www.QuickChangeArtist.com. For information about Dr. Brinkman's keynotes and seminars, visit www.RickBrinkman.com. To learn more about their work together, visit www.TheRicks.com.